The Ultimate D
ANTHOLOGY
for the working drummer
Steve Houghton

TABLE OF CONTENTS

FOREWORD

This book is designed to provide the drummer with a diverse collection of *real* drum charts that are representative of those found in the workplace. Because each chart looks different, it is important to understand the reading format of each specific chart.

Performance areas covered are Big Band, Small Group, Live Shows, Broadway Shows, Studio Work, Dance Jobs and Cruise Ships.

Each performance area is discussed in terms of responsibilities, challenges, expectations, awareness and problem areas. In addition, each piece of music is analyzed and practical performance suggestions are provided. Most of the charts have accompaniment tracks for demonstration and/or performance purposes.

After working through all the different performance areas, the drummer will have a clearer idea of what types of reading demands are found in the workplace. In addition, the drummer will learn how to play what is appropriate for each job and how to fit effectively into any musical situation.

ABOUT THE RECORDING

The CD recording serves two purposes. First, it will provide the player with accompaniment tracks to the charts, so the drummer can hear the interpretation while seeing the original part. The recordings have been mixed with the drums on the left channel so that they can be dialed out, enabling the the student to substitute his/her own playing.

Second, the player will hear short demonstrations of interpretation ideas, problem spots, groove suggestions and other concepts that will aid him/her in understanding the music. Because many of the charts call for a big band or orchestra, we've recreated the music with a trio. Nevertheless, the player should be able to play out and catch the figures with the same excitement as if playing in a large ensemble.

INTRODUCTION!

I find that many drummers, regardless of age, have decided that learning to read music is either too hard or not important. Well, I'm not prepared to settle an age-old debate merely by writing this book. However, what I would like to do is offer a different approach to reading drum charts by providing you with a vast collection of music and some performance ideas that, hopefully, will inspire some of you to "bite the bullet" and learn to read. The old line "Reading Is Fun" takes on new meaning here, for the types of jobs available to readers are varied, challenging and, frequently, lucrative.

One reason reading gets a "bum rap" is that drummers often can't understand the transition from snare drum books to drumset charts. They look very different and they are! The major difference is that drum charts must be interpreted while snare drum music is basically played "as is." Another source of confusion is that there are many different chart-reading formats, and as you will see, each one looks totally different.

Chart reading is challenging because it brings together three crucial elements of drumming: technique, style and reading/interpretation. To play any given chart, you must have the ability to read the rhythms/figures, the knowledge of that particular style and the technique to execute it. This is a tall order for any drummer, so it's a good idea to devise a system of practice that brings all of these ideas together. Finally, I've found that utilizing the following three concepts in your practice routine will help develop your reading skills:

- Always Count—out loud if necessary

- Don't Stop—if you make a mistake, just keep going for continuity.

- Read Something Every Day— daily repetition using different music is essential.

This collection is just the tip of the iceberg in terms of what you might face on a job, but it will give you a broad base of exposure to the types of music played by drummers every day. Welcome to the world of the reading drumset player!

ABOUT THE AUTHOR

Internationally respected as a jazz drummer, percussionist, clinician and educator, Steve Houghton has shared both stage and studio with renowned jazz and pop artists including Joe Henderson, Maureen McGovern, Arturo Sandoval, Gary Burton, Billy Childs, Scott Henderson and Bob Florence. A Wisconsin native, Houghton received his first acclaim at age 20 as drummer with Woody Herman's Young Thundering Herd. He was chosen for The Herd while a member of the University of North Texas One O'Clock Lab Band, with which he recorded *Lab '75*, the band's first Grammy-nominated album, comprised of Lyle Mays arrangements.

After two years with The Herd, Houghton polished his reading skills in the Dallas studios for four years, then moved to California where he quickly established himself through his tenure with Toshiko Akiyoshi. In 1980, a last-minute call to substitute for Freddie Hubbard's drummer evolved into a two-year association. By the mid-'80s, Houghton, a busy Los Angeles studio musician, was writing, teaching at area universities and performing with symphony orchestras as a featured guest percussionist, activities he continues to pursue today.

Houghton's recordings as leader include *Steve Houghton* (Signature Series, Mesa Bluemoon), *Remembrances* (Warner Bros.) and *Windsong* (SHPERC Records). He also may be heard on *The Music of Pat Metheny & Lyle Mays with Bob Curnow's LA Big Band* (MAMA Foundation). Houghton is the author of more than 20 composite educational publications, including *The Contemporary Rhythm Section* (text and video series), *Essential Styles* (play-along series) and his most recent collection, *MasterTracks* (play-along improvisation series).

Houghton is a member of the Percussive Arts Society board of directors and co-chairman of the International Association of Jazz Educators percussion division. He endorses Pearl/Adams, Zildjian, Calato, Innovative Percussion and Remo products.

CREDITS

Project Editor: Dave Black
Artwork/layout: Kim Kasabian & Bruce Goldes
Engineer: Talley Sherwood
Recorded at: Stagg Street Studios
Bass/arranger: Tom Warrington
Piano/synthesizer: Tom Ranier

Special thanks to:
Pati Graham, Dave Black, Maureen McGovern, Matt Harris, Sammy Nestico, Mark Nestico, Jeff Jarvis, C.L. Barnhouse, Bob Breithaupt and Les Hooper.

GLOSSARY OF TERMS

The following is a comprehensive list of drumset chart terms found in the performance areas covered in this book.

– 1
Cutoff or release on beat 1.

Accel.
Accelerando: get faster.

Ad lib.
Fake or improvise.

A Tempo, Tempo 1, Tempo Primo
Play the original tempo.

Backbeat, Heavy 2 and 4
Accent, usually with the left hand, the 2nd and 4th beats.

    (arrow) Begin at arrow.

B.D., Bs. Dr.
Bass drum.

Bell
Usually the bell of the cymbal or cowbell.

Bell cue
Single note or octave on orchestra bells.

Big 2
Half-time feel accent on beat 3.

Bigger
Play louder or stronger.

Blocks, Temp. Blks.
Temple blocks.

Blues
Music with 12-16 bar structure or form.

Bone or T-bone
Trombone.

Bows
Special music to be played during a performer's bows.

Br.
Brass.

Break
Stop playing even though the musical form continues.

Bridge
In AABA song form, the B section; different section that follows repeated A section and precedes final A section.

Br., Brush
Brushes.

C.B.
Cowbell.

Chaser
Music that "chases" an act as it leaves the stage.

Chorus
One complete time through the form.

Closed or Tight Sock
Hold cymbals of hi-hat together with foot while hands play the rhythm.

  Coda sign.

Colla Voce
With the voice/singer.

Cresc.
Crescendo; get louder.

Cross-stick
Stick played on rim, with the bead of the stick resting on the head.

Cues
Words, actions or music that will help identify your place or entrance.

"Cut," Cut-off
The conductor or performer indicates a stop.

Cut to
An indication to skip to another place.

Cym., Cymb.
Cymbal.

D.C.
Da capo back to the head or beginning.

Decresc.
Decrescendo; get softer.

Dictated
Conducted.

Dim.
Diminuendo; get softer.

Dixie
Dixieland style.

Dome
Play on the dome of the cymbal.

D.B.
Play on the downbeat with no count-off.

  (*segno*, sign) The sign that you go to in a D.S.

Dbl. x feel
Double-time feel; play a beat that feels twice as fast.

Dbl. x swing
Double-time swing feel; play a swing tempo that feels twice as fast as the original.

Encore
Material performed after applause at the end of a show.

Ens.
Ensemble.

Entr'acte
Music at the beginning of an act that serves as an interlude before action begins on stage.

 Eyeglasses; watch for this spot.

Fade
Fade or die away.

 **Fermata, or hold**
Sustain the note or rest over which it's placed.

Fill
"Fill-in."

Four Beat
"Flat four" feel, generally with the bass drum played on all four beats.

In Four, In 4
Generally means the ride cymbal plays a driving quarter-note concept.

Gospel
Rhythm in 12/8 time or with triplet feel in 4/4 time.

G.P.
Grand pause.

H.H.
Time on the hi-hat.

Half x feel
A beat which feels half as fast as the original tempo.

Heavy 2 & 4
Accent, usually with the left hand, on the 2nd and 4th beats.

Horns
Horns are playing the rhythm indicated.

"In 1," "In 2," "In 3," "In 4"
One, two, three or four beats per bar.

Intro.
Introduction or beginning of tune.

Jungle
Play repetitive pattern on tom-toms.

Latin
Play Latin style.

"Lay Back"
Relax the time feel.

Lead In
Fill into.

L'istesso tempo
Same time.

L.T.T., L.T.
Low tom.

L.V.
Let vibrate.

Mar., Mrcs.
Maracas.

Military
March-like style.

M.T.T., High Tom
Mounted, high tom.

"Open up"
Get louder or busier.

"Out Chorus"
Last chorus of the tune. Is usually louder and more driving.

Pno.
Piano.

Rall.
Rallentando; slow down.

// "Railroad tracks;" a stop in the music.

Reprise
The repeat of music played earlier.

"Ricky-Tic"
Light, triplet style—often accompanying dance.

"Ride," R.C.
Ride cymbal.

Rim
Rim of drum.

Rimshot
One stick played on the other, with the bead of the left stick resting on the drum, creating a "gunshot" effect.

Rit.
Ritard; slow down.

Safety
A vamp whose length may vary in every performance.

Sax., Sx.
Saxophone.

Segue
Move from one section or piece of music to another without pause.

Shake, Shakr.
Shaker.

Shout Chorus
The last, and usually loudest, chorus of the tune.

"Show 2"
A "boom-chick" style found in show music.

Simile
Continue the same groove.

Sn. Dr., S.D., Sn.
Snare drum.

"Soft-Shoe"
To accompany in dance style; generally on rim of woodblock.

Soli
A solo played by more than one, usually by a section in a big band.

Solo
Playing or soloing with accompaniment.

Spiritual
Slow triplet-style (12/8) piece of music.

"Straight 8th"
Feel in which each eighth note receives equal value; do not swing eighth notes.

"Straight Time"
Similar or same.

Stripper Beat
Type of beat with heavy accents usually on 2 and 4 with loud tom toms.

Strut
Tight feel, accent on 2 and 4.

Stx., Stix, To Stix.
Sticks.

"Swing"
Play "Swing" feel.

Tacet
Do not play.

Tag
"Tagging on an ending." A short extension of the form that brings the music to a conclusion.

Tbone, Bone
Trombone.

Tamb.
Tambourine.

Temp. Blks, Blocks
Temple blocks.

Tempo 1, Tempo Primo, A Tempo
Play the original tempo.

Timb.
Timbales.

Time
Rhythm that is employed by the drummer in a particular style.

Tog.
Together.

Tom, Toms, T.T.
Tom-toms.

Tri., Trgl.
Triangle.

Trpt.
Trumpet.

Tutti
All play together.

"Two Beat" "Two feel."
Emphasis with light bass drum on beats 1 and 3:

"Two Feel"
Or "2-Feel" (See "Two Beat" above).

2xo
Play background figure the second time only.

Unis.
Unison.

Vamp
Repeat a measure or number of measures until the conductor cues to continue.

V.S.
Volti subito; usually meaning a fast page turn.

"Walk"
Straight time, much as the "walking bass."

WB, W.B., W.Blk.
Woodblock.

X (1x, 2x, etc.)
The number of times a passage is repeated; 4x = 4 times, etc.

Chapter 1
BIG BAND

The demands on a big band drummer have changed considerably through the years, as this music has become more stylistically diverse. That said, the drummer's role is still the same: provide excitement, kick the band, play dynamics, support the soloists and play the style.

One common problem with big band charts is that they can be unclear at best. The drummer must be able to quickly determine who is playing each figure so he/she can know how and when to setup/fill. The drummer functions behind either a section of the band or the entire ensemble.

Behind a section: While keeping time, the drummer will catch occasional section figures, which are rhythms played by one section of the band. When playing these figures, the ride cymbal should not be interrupted while the figure is played by either the snare drum or bass drum.

Behind the ensemble: An ensemble figure (a rhythm played by the entire band) needs to be caught but also setup (filled into) by the drums. The time-keeping on the ride cymbal might have to be interrupted if both hands are needed to setup the figures.

One of the drummer's biggest concerns is catching ensemble figures while keeping the groove going. Latin charts seem to be especially challenging. In all styles, however, the drums must find a way to camouflage the kicks within the time-keeping, which will allow for a continuous flow in the music.

A crucial, yet misunderstood, role is that of supporting the horn soloists throughout a chart; this requires the drummer to react like a small-group player. Communication between the drummer and the pianist, bassist and soloist can best be honed in a small-group setting.

PERFORMANCE NOTES/SUGGESTIONS

Basie-Straight Ahead

This is one of the most famous Sammy Nestico arrangements written for the Count Basie band. Oddly enough, it is played at a wide variety of tempos, so be flexible. The cross-stick becomes an invaluable tool in this context. Again, as with the many Basie charts starting with a piano solo, the hi-hat seems to offer the perfect support.

Understand that the fill material changes as the tempo increases or decreases. The band figures need to be played very crisply in this style. It's interesting—and highly unusual—that Nestico took the time to orchestrate some of the snare drum/bass drum hits, but they sound very good, so give 'em a go!

Ya' Gotta Try

This is classic Basie; the chart starts out with a piano solo at a brisk tempo. This is often played or interpreted on the hi-hat to allow for a gradual build in the piece. At letter A, one might choose to go to a ride cymbal in order to support the new soloist. At letter B, those section figures could be interpreted with the bass drum, then a busy ensemble section begins. The two-bar rest is for the soloist, but it is a common practice to fill on the second bar to set up the soloist.

Letters C and D are tenor solos, so they should "burn" right along using interplay or cross-stick. The sendoffs into the various solos should be played with power. At letter G, fill

material could go one of two ways: triplets could be used if the tempo is not too fierce; otherwise, eighth notes must be used.

Letter I can also be interpreted two ways: first, as "kicks" with the drummer catching the rhythms, then as a "chop wood" section in which you don't concern yourself with the "kicks" but simply hit strong backbeats.

I've Got You Under My Skin

This classic big band chart is from the library of the late, great Frank Sinatra and will teach you both patience and taste. This chart emphasizes establishing a sophisticated groove by using a light hi-hat for an extended period of time and a light bass drum to match what is happening in the bass line. The challenge for the drummer is to be patient and not clutter the first part of the song.

The arrangement stays in a kind of two feel until letter C, where it goes to four. Check out the simple, swinging ensemble figures notated above the staff. These figures shouldn't be played too strongly, as they are supporting the bridge of the song. The chart really opens up at letter E, so get the energy going before that section with some time-keeping that really mixes it up and builds tension.

The D. S. takes you back to the bridge with the driving four feel, and then the coda brings you to the original hi-hat groove at the beginning. Have fun with "Ol' Blue Eyes!"

I'll Never Smile Again

The slow tempo of this chart makes trying to maintain the initial tempo quite a challenge. Bands can either drag this type of a piece or rush it to death, so be prepared for anything. Playing the horn figures simply takes musicality and grace, so be careful not to be heavy-handed. The setups should be musical and not intrude on the chart too much (not too busy or long). The groove you develop with the bass is the foundation for the entire piece, so focus on that relationship.

Magic Flea

This chart really flies by, so it's important that the drummer understand the use of cross-stick (beats 2 & 4 or just 4) in order to hold the band together. Know that the use of the bass drum at key phrase points will help the band a great deal. A clear, strong ride beat is essential, along with a clear sense of the phrasing (filling in the right spots).

The fills in this chart are going to be either very fast triplets or bright eighth notes, whichever sounds more musical. Try to construct concise fills that will set up the next figure.

Mambo de Memo

This chart is a great example of a contemporary big band mambo. When Latin music is played in published form, the groove for the chart is often laid out in the first four to eight bars, and it is suggested that the drummer play it throughout the tune.

At bar 9, where the band "hits" occur, try to catch the "hits" while keeping the groove going—which can be very challenging in Latin music. The interpretation can even be somewhat loose in order to keep everything together, and can utilize triplets as well as eighth notes.

A traditional salsa setting would have the drummer playing a more pronounced role in relation to other percussionists. In this chart, however, the drums can be a bit more active. At bar 41, the piano ostinato begins, so the drummer must try to link-up to that rhythm. This is why a thorough knowledge of clave (rhythmic skeleton) and how it is applied to piano ostinatos is mandatory in a Latin setting. In this instance, the rumba clave is used in the 2-3 form because the piano accents follow that pattern.

Example:

At bar 65, the tune opens up a bit, so a move to the ride cymbal makes sense musically. Two bars before 89, we have the send-off, which must be strong. The rest of the chart follows the same concept... Enjoy!

Basie-Straight Ahead

Composed & Arranged by Sammy Nestico

Basie-Straight Ahead

Ya' Gotta Try

By Sammy Nestico

Ya' Gotta Try

DRUMS

I'VE GOT YOU UNDER MY SKIN

Arr. by Torrie Zito

Track 3

Track 4

DRUMS

I'LL NEVER SMILE AGAIN

Arr. by Torrie Zito

Magic Flea

by Sammy Nestico

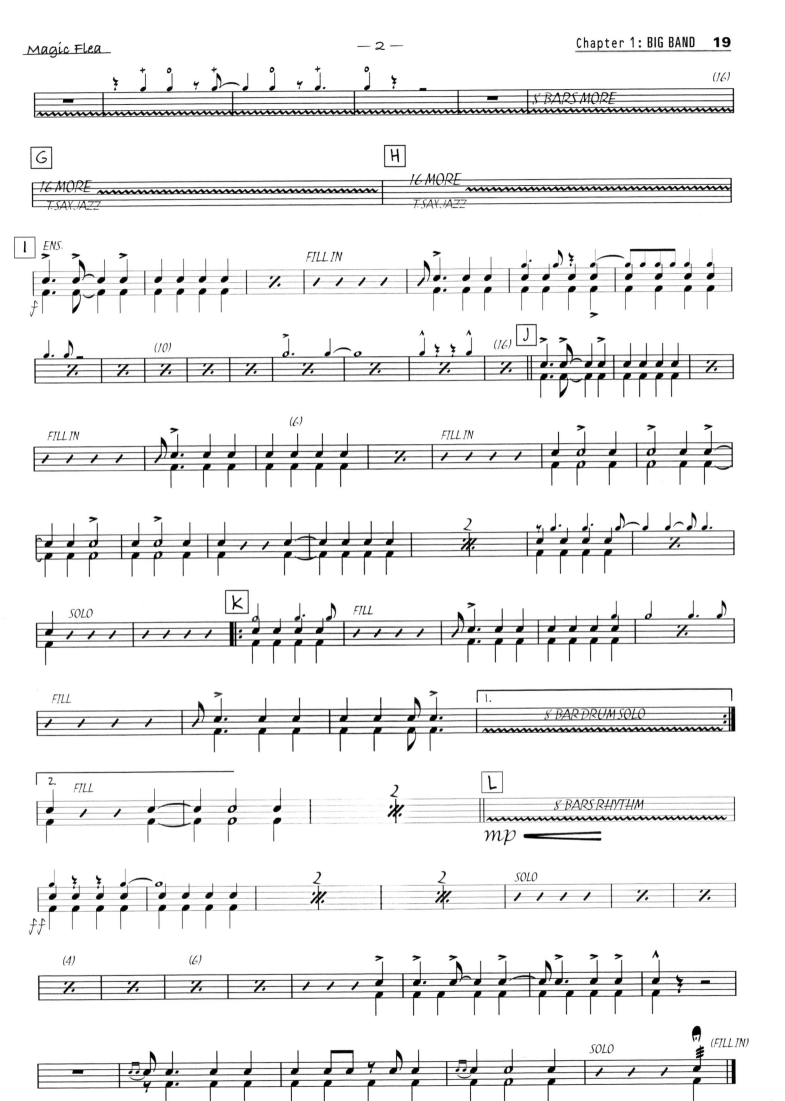

Magic Flea

Track 6

DRUMS

by Matt Harris

Mambo De Memo

Mambo De Memo

Chapter 2
SMALL GROUP

A small-group setting may or may not use charts. I've found that about half the time they do. The main requirements in this setting are to play good time, blend with the group and nail the style. Often, drummers overplay in a small group. A small group must work together like a classical chamber group in which no single member forces or dictates the style.

When playing from lead sheets, the drummer must understand and follow the chord symbols since they are vital to the interpretation of the tune. A drummer who understands the form and harmonic progressions will be able to get "inside" the music.

When catching or playing figures in a small group, always pay close attention to dynamics and don't overpower the group with the setups. The concept of subtle setups in a small group is similar to the way in which strong fills are used in a big band.

PERFORMANCE NOTES/SUGGESTIONS

Bogus Blues

This tune is just a simple 12-bar blues form with an interesting head (or melody) that should be interpreted by the drummer.

When playing a blues, the most important element is keeping track of the 12-bar form. After the solos, the drummer usually trades "fours" with the other soloists, after which the "out" melody is played again, probably twice.

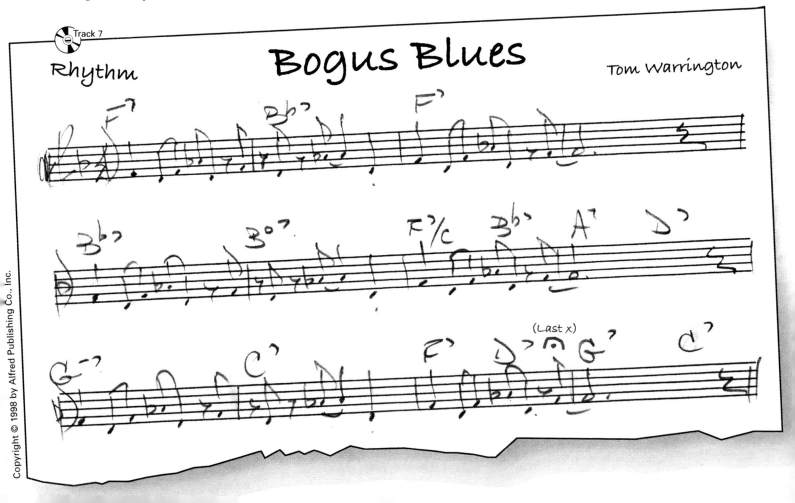

Rio Rhythm

This is a common jazz song form (AABA) consisting of 32 bars, and is based on the tune "I Got Rhythm." On the bridge, notice how the harmonic rhythm slows down, which means the drums can open up a bit. Again, it is important that the drummer know this form inside and out so he/she can better accompany the melody and solos. When and if the drum solo occurs, be ready to trade "eights" with the band. This version calls for a samba feel, but the tune is most often played with a bright swing feel, so be flexible with the stylistic interpretations.

Track 8

The Audition

This chart has just about everything in it, so be prepared. It starts off by playing swing on the hi-hat, then segues at bar 18 to a light samba, so make sure the setup fill is clear.

The next transition fill, at bar 73, is also important. Shortly thereafter, the drummer is called upon to count off the new tempo (♩=132), so have the tempo in your head, keeping in mind that a double-time swing section is coming at bar 127, with a transition fill preceding it at bar 126.

Lots of figures are in the last section, so be efficient and not too busy with your fills. Be ready for the "take it home" ending—nice and big, lots of triplets. Have fun with this multi-styles/multi-transition workout.

The Audition

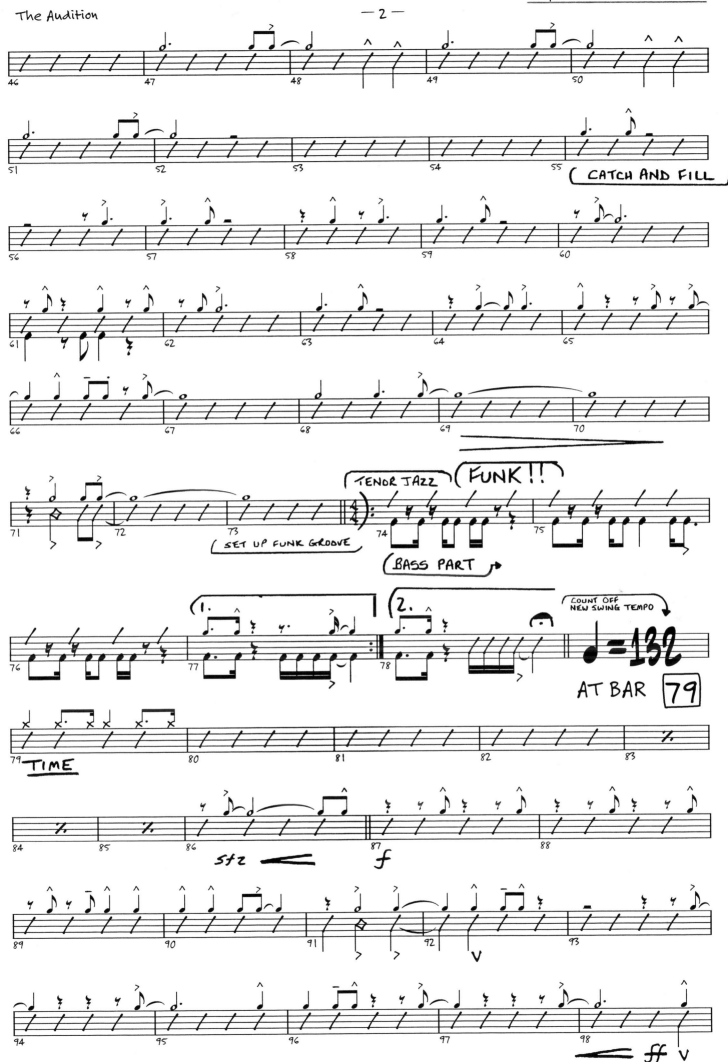

— 3 —

The Audition

Fall Leaves

The chord changes and form resemble the familiar jazz standard, "Autumn Leaves." Jazz standards are often played in styles completely different from the original, so be open-minded, flexible and creative. This particular version is in a hip-hop style. Be aware of the bass part, because it will help to determine your bass drum part.

Track 10

Fall Leaves

Rhythm
Hip-Hop

Tom Warrington

Funk

This track starts with only the hi-hat and some subtle filling. The bass drum enters at bar 5 and continues until the groove finally develops at letter A.

At the bridge, go to the ride cymbal for contrast, utilize a bit more syncopation and catch the pushes at bars 7 and 8 of letter B.

Letter C is a slight variation on the original groove which picks up again at letter D. The ending needs to be played precisely.

Track 11

Funk

Tom Warrington & Steve Houghton

Voyage Home

This tune has what some might call a "Maiden Voyage" feel, which can be described as a hypnotic, straight-eighth, cymbal-based groove with some repetitive kicks. It is vital that one listen to songs that employ this rhythmic concept, including the Herbie Hancock recording of "Maiden Voyage." This is a rather long song in terms of form and the number of bars, so learn, memorize and, finally, hear the tune.

Chapter 3
BROADWAY SHOWS

The skills required of a Broadway show drummer are numerous and diverse, but most critical is the ability to follow a conductor. The drummer must develop good rapport with the conductor and totally understand his/her beat patterns and gestures (indicating louder, softer, faster, slower, etc.). Because the conductor has to accommodate singers and dancers, the tempos or performance situations may vary from night to night, which requires the drummer to be extremely flexible.

A typical Broadway show drum part contains many different terms or directions in the music (colla voce, word cues, etc.) and sound effects or auxiliary percussion parts (gunshot, woodblock, tri., etc.). These parts cannot be freely interpreted as in a jazz big band chart because the part reflects dance moves, stage effects or facial expressions. In addition, Broadway composers have a very clear idea of when they want to hear hi-hat as opposed to ride cymbal, and those places usually are clearly marked.

Another problem is handling page turns, as some of the parts can have as many as 10–15 pages (I've been there!). One must figure out when to turn pages and how to set up a page layout (book style works the best).

Perhaps one of the most important demands on a "pit" drummer is the ability to play something exactly the same way night after night. Singers and dancers depend on a high level of consistency from the orchestra, especially from the drums, as they frequently must listen for fills to guide them to their entrances.

Finally, Broadway music is famous for not having traditional grooves that can be catagorized as jazz, samba, bossa, etc. In fact, more often than not, this type of music often contains anti-grooves or odd grooves that simply fit the music or the lyric, which sometimes last only two or three bars. It can be very challenging to make these grooves feel good without changing them into something more hip or modern sounding, which in effect would be inappropriate for the show.

Act II, Scene 13

Although this vintage Broadway chart has no accompaniment track, it's included here to illustrate the range of instruments possible within a given cue. The beginning

tempo slows down four bars later. The next seven bars are counted by following the vocals (Colla voce; see glossary).

The tempo starts again at bar 12 on bongos, goes to a cymbal

at 21 with a meter change, then back to bongos. From 54 to the end, timpani, bongos, cymbal and drumset (brushes) are played.

"Bubbles"

The style of this chart includes elements of exotic dance or "stripper music" and utilizes rimshots, tom-toms and cymbal chokes to support the rather humorous, yet sexy, dance moves on stage.   (Popular in the 1920s and 30s, the Bubble Dance was performed under low lights by a shapely, supposedly nude female who used a large ball (bubble) to cover key anatomical parts as she danced.)

There are big band elements in this piece but also a lot of humor, so the playing should never get too jazzy. At bar 29, a comedy bit on stage must be caught by simply feeling it, so be flexible. Since you probably won't be able to see the stage, you must follow the conductor and/or use your ears and a keen sense of timing. The tempo at bar 37 plods along unevenly, ending with a quick cymbal choke at bar 44.

Vaudeville Chase

This is an excerpt from a "Keystone Cops" vaudeville type of piece, so be prepared to play sound effects and catch pratfalls (exaggerated falls or mishaps) on the stage. Instruments used in this cue include a police whistle, woodblock, siren, duck call, cowbell,

pop gun and drumset. On all snare drum and bass drum work, it is acceptable to use a very light quarter- or eighth-note hi-hat to hold things together.

At bars 51–63, several sound effects come one right after another, so be ready. Next is a cymbal roll that reflects some-

one almost falling off a cliff, with cymbal swells adding to the drama.

The original chart continues for 10 more pages, which is typical, so you must have endurance and stay intensely focused on the overall direction and pacing when playing this style.

The Coup

This piece begins in a military style that transitions into a medium rock feel at bar 53. The solos at bars 66, 68 and 70 must be in the right style and played in time; be careful not to overplay the solos.

At bar 73, there is a written cue to alert the playing of the cymbal. Bars 74–77 have a shuffle feel, which use ride cymbal and snare drum. Although the recording ends at bar 78, the chart continues with a variety of additional reading challenges.

Chapter 4
LIVE SHOWS

Live shows are some of the most enjoyable jobs to play because of their variety, but they can also be some of the most stressful because they are live. Included in this category are circuses, rodeos, Vegas-style acts, ice (skating) shows, variety shows, civic musicals, industrial shows, live TV (Tonight Show, David Letterman, etc.), TV awards shows (Academy Awards, Grammy Awards, etc.) and pops concerts. The typical live show might bring together jazz, Broadway, small group, big band and rock 'n' roll drumming, all in one evening. For this reason, stylistic versatility is a must, along with a keen ability to follow a conductor.

The charts can have elements similar to Broadway or big band music in which the drums hold everything together and provide excitement, so the techniques employed in those styles will be most useful. If singers or dancers are involved, then the proper support must be offered (cross-stick, simple time, easy fills, etc.).

I've found that the live-show setting is not the place to be transparent or subtle. The band needs direction and leadership from the drum chair with fills/transition setups that are clear and bold.

Even play-ons and play-offs, used frequently at awards shows, must be played with authority and excitement, although they may last only three to five seconds. The style must be instantly understood with the tempo preset, since there may not be time for a count-off.

Keep in mind that each situation demands unique skills from the drummer—and that no two charts ever look the same.

PERFORMANCE NOTES/SUGGESTIONS

Pops Singer
This chart really puts the drummer through the paces, starting with a march and transitioning to a samba feel while catching band figures.

After the fermata at bar 46, the drums set the new tempo until bar 79 where it goes to a driving "four" feel. Pay attention at bar 89, where the 5/4 time starts. Bar 98 sets up the Swing 4 again. The next section is typical of pops vocal charts in which the styles change rapidly (Swing 4, Tango, March, 2-beat, Shuffle).

I can't say enough about the ability to start a style without a count-off and to have the correct tempo in your head. It is a good idea to practice "nailing" the proper tempo (check with a metronome) as well as transitioning from style-to-style.

Circus March
This is one of the most famous circus marches of all time, one that everyone has heard probably a million times. The playing of a piece like this is pretty straightforward, in that you play a march style. However, its use with circus acts demands you put even more energy into the performance, catching jugglers, acrobats, clowns, etc., so make good use of the crashes.

At the trio, there are different instrument choices you can make to provide contrast, like playing on the rim of the snare drum or on a woodblock.

Be prepared for drastic tempo changes, as on the last refrain; it often goes into double-time, so be ready. Also, prepare to play all of the cymbal crashes, as you are really taking the place of three percussionists. The rolls in this chart need to be very clean and precise, performed with energy and direction.

Circus March

K. L. King

Play-Ons/Play-Offs

Many times a play-on will have a word that describes the character of the cue (i.e., elegant, sexy, cool, funky, etc.). These will actually come in quite handy.

Play-On #1 Track 18

This is a typical play-on that starts with a cymbal roll leading into the full ensemble, so play out and don't be bashful. The drums should play the unison rhythm with the horns; a slight fill into the second bar will help hold things together. This particular play-on slows down (ritards) just a bit at the end. Unison figures could be played on toms or on a combination of snare, bass and cymbals.

Play-On #2 Track 19

This play-on calls for a swing feel, meaning "not too jazzy but take care of business." Again, this cue starts with a fill that should set up the tempo and energy of the play-on. Remember, nothing is worse than a setup that doesn't properly foreshadow what's ahead.

Play-On #3 Track 20

This is a sexy, bossa style, so have a nice smooth cymbal ready to go. Don't overplay the figures in this one since they are subtle. This play-on also slows down (ritards) musically in the last bar.

Play-Off #1 Track 21

Occasionally, play-offs are the same as play-ons, but can frequently be different. This is a short little show-feel that you might hear on a variety show at the end of a comedy skit. It should never get too hip and should have a nice button on the last note, played in time.

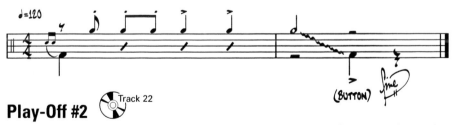

Play-Off #2 Track 22

This is a funky cue that starts out grooving. The first two bass drum notes are with the band, so play them as is. In fact, the whole measure is the exact horn lick, so make it feel good when you catch the hit into the last bar.

Show Medley

This chart is part of a medley of tunes from a film. Although it looks like a straight-ahead drum part, you are playing it with a 100-piece orchestra, so it can feel really bulky. I like to say it compares to "pulling a herd of semis." Anyway, a good interpretation is to play the part (good style, kicks, fills, transitions) with an eye on keeping everything very broad and easy to hear.

The distance factor when playing with an orchestra (where trumpets are 50 feet away) is a real acoustical challenge. Also, conductors for these types of concerts don't always have a jazz/pops background, which sometimes results in stiff, unswinging movements. Be forewarned that you'll always be playing too loudly for the string players, so don't take it personally.

Another Opener

This chart comes from a variety show benefit where there was a "Hollywood" theme, hence the big intro with the timpani/tom-tom roll. Apparently, there wasn't time to copy a drum part so you're reading off a chord sheet. The chords will actually spell out the drum part, along with reading the rests and bass notes. Remember, this is an opener, which needs lots of excitement and energy. Don't hold back!

Track 24

ANOTHER OPENER

ARRANGED BY B. K.

Chapter 5
CRUISE SHIPS

Cruise ship music presents an interesting set of challenges, not the least of which is the physical condition of the charts. Often, the artists and their music have traveled extensively from cruise-to-cruise; therefore, the charts can be messy, cluttered and confusing. In this instance, try to find the latest (freshest) set of markings on the part and follow those instructions. The pianist/conductor will know the act, so it's a good idea to huddle with him/her before the rehearsal.

A student of mine who ended up on a ship for many years wrote the following in a letter to me: "As simple as it is, I can't stress the importance of being able to play a 'show two' at fast tempos for two or three minutes while catching a few crashes. I've found that show charts—although similar to big band charts—often segue, change tempos, time signatures and styles. They all require the drummer to follow a conductor who counts off a tempo that may not remain the same until the end of the piece."

In a cruise ship setting, there is frequently just such a conductor whom you must follow through music that covers a wide range of styles, so be prepared. Good, solid show styles, jazz, rock and Latin styles are a must. The hip jazz and Afro-Cuban material you've worked on probably won't be needed. Sorry.

For your enlightenment and amusement, I've included a realistic "cue sheet" that was taken directly from a ship. It isn't pretty, but it describes an act sequence that the drummer must follow and reproduce. So, keep your place, use your eyes and ears, play the style, watch the conductor—and don't get seasick!

Nagila Bows

This is a very common tempo and style for bows. Again, the main ingredient is energy, since the show has concluded and the act is coming back out to accept more applause.

Bow cue sheets always repeat as needed (ad nauseum!) until the band is cued to stop by the conductor. Take no prisoners! You're through for the day!

 Track 25

"Zardos the Violinist"

For some reason, there seems to be a fair number of marimba and violin soloists performing on cruise ships. This tune is the type you might find with these kinds of acts.

The two fermatas in the beginning are conducted, followed by a long hold and then a cut-off. There are directions to follow the soloist's movements until letter A, where the soloist finally sets the tempo, which is brisk. The rimshots support movements on the stage. A strong show two-beat is needed. *A note of caution:* don't be too alarmed if the soloist gets one or two beats ahead of the band; it happens all the time. If this should happen, it is best for the band to remain together as a unit, so stick to your guns and put it where it should be. The soloist will adjust to a strong rhythm section.

Used with Permission.

España Carni—Escape Artist

This particular chart presents a few challenges; the first is its use of percussion terms in German. *Castagnetten*—castanets, *Kl. Trommel*—snare drum, *Gran Trommel*—bass drum and *Becken*—cymbal.

After translating the terms you can see this is really a percussion section part, not a drumset part. If you don't have machine castanets, substitutes include the rim of the snare drum or tom, or the shell of the floor tom.

You'll have to choreograph how to play the castanets and snare at the same time, but it can be done. "Viva la España!"

Arranged by
Tom Warrington

España Carni
Paso-Doble

Spanischer Zigeunertanz

Batteria
(Drums)

"The Carlsons"—Juggling Act
The whole purpose of the music in this setting is to create energy and tension, catch tricks or movement, and create moods (scary, exciting, frantic, mysterious, etc.). This cue happens to call for lots of energy, starting with a snare drum roll going to a quick show-two feel with a few crashes and sound effects thrown in. There is nothing subtle about this style; you must watch the act to coordinate the hits.

(I played an act once where the juggler insisted that I "catch everything, Mr. Drummer." By accident, he dropped a hat, so I caught it with a loud rimshot. In fact, he dropped several hats, and I caught them all, to the band's delight. Needless to say, that was not what he had in mind.)

Track 28

Bernie's Magic Act

This "cue sheet" is common on cruise ships and is used mostly for magicians and jugglers.

There is not one drum notation on the sheet, which leaves the drummer to follow only visual and aural cues. (Don't fall asleep!) As you can see, a good snare drum roll and a rimshot are necessities.

- ENTRANCE: "WILD ABOUT HARRY" (letter B)

LINKING RINGS:

- RIMSHOT as I count rings. EXCEPT 8th RING

- TOUCH CHIMES each time I link one ring onto another ring. (2 times)
  3 RIM SHOTS AS HE SLAPS RING WITH AUDIENCE ASSISTANT
- GLISS UP ON CHIMES as one ring passes thru other 3 rings.

- RIMSHOT (♪♫) on turnover. (NOTE: audience with be shouting "Paquet!")

- DRUMROLL - My Cue.

- CHORD when all rings are linked in a chain
  (CUE: "The 8 Golden Rings of China!...")

- CHORD (again) after I link all rings onto one ring.
  (CUE: "The 8 Golden Rings of China!")

NEEDLE THRU BALLOON:

- "UP, UP AND AWAY" — IMMEDIATELY as I blow up balloon - I'll Cut.

- DRUMROLL — My Cue

- "TA-DA BIT" - At end of routine, stand and shout "Ta-Da!"
  (as balloon pops).

FLASH: USE MALLETS
- LIGHT CYMBAL ROLL as I pull out lit match and light bowl — build as flash paper burns.

- CHORD after flash.

- CHORD (again) as I thank volunteer.

PING- PONG BALL BIT:

- DRUMROLL - My Cue.

- CRASH when ball lands on my nose — NO CHORD.

$100 BILL TRICK:

- "MONEY - MONEY" or "I'M IN THE MONEY" (Piano Only) on (CUE: "I need $100 Bucks!...") — CUT when spectator reaches edge of stage.

- RIMSHOT (♪♫) on (CUE: "What you have just done is illegal!")

- LIGHT DRUMROLL as I light lighter — continue until 3rd envelope is burned.

- BIG DRUMROLL (SNARE) as spectator opens his/her envelope.
  FADE-OUT ROLL WHEN HE PUTS FLAME OUT
- CHORD on (CUE: "Well, let's give him/her a big hand for coming up here!")

- BIG DRUMROLL (TYMP) - My Cue (NOTE: I'll Cut)

Chapter 6
STUDIO WORK

The performance area called "studio work" includes many different elements: TV, film, record dates, live show pre-record, jingles, radio IDs, industrial films, demos, etc. For this reason, a studio player needs a wealth of experience from which to draw.

As in other areas, the terms used commonly in the studio differ from those in the real world. For example, the term "–1" simply means "off" or "release on beat 1." Knowing these terms is critical in a recording session, a setting where silence is essential. The drummer must be ready to read from a variety of parts and must be able to perform without much, if any, rehearsal—and without asking lots of questions.

Also, the ability to make things "feel good" very quickly is a must. Making a 5-, 15-, 30-, or 60-second spot or piece of music sparkle is a real challenge. There is no time for a groove to develop, and reading mistakes are frowned upon. Players must be exceptionally accurate readers to receive repeated calls for studio work, which can be highly lucrative.

Playing with a click-track and playing while listening through headphones are skills that must become second nature. Occasionally, the drummer will have to replace a drum part or play over an existing track, which can be highly challenging.

TV Sports Promo

When you're told you'll be recording sports promos, that means just one thing—macho energy! The drummer's role in these types of cues is vital; fills and cymbal crashes must match the action onscreen. The fills must be bold and not too slick or busy. Many times, the rhythm section will be recorded first and horns will be recorded later in the day, so it's essential for the drummer to understand big band concepts and play as though the horns were in the room. If your playing isn't powerful enough, there's no chance to fix it later.

M 11—Movie Underscore

This cue is from a scene in a movie; it starts off in a funk-type groove and eventually transitions to an R&B strut feel. The reading format is a master rhythm part, which doesn't contain a drum part *per se*. Again, the bass part tells the story, along with punches in the piano part. Understand that this probably will be buried under dialogue or sound effects, but play it well and have fun anyway.

Track 30

M 11-Movie Underscore

Cartoons

"Toons" are always fun to record, especially if you can see the action while recording. Imagining how it will sound on TV will help you define your role, which is "nuts and bolts," or "play what's on the page and keep it simple." The styles of the following cartoon cues include a 12/8 march and a bright "show two" feel.

In the march, the drummer is called upon to play splashed hi-hat with bass drum to create a marching band effect. This march needs to have an attitude vs. a heavy, military march. One phrasing note—it helps the energy and direction to slightly accent the second note of each triplet as such:

Track 31

TOON No. 1

MARCH FEEL   LES HOOPER

Toon No. 2

The "show two" is a typical example of a "madcap" cartoon sequence with lots of action.

The groove at bar 3 has to be light and clean, and the roll sequence must be precise and forward-moving. The low tom in bar 21 is a common occurrence that supports a movement onscreen. Have fun catching "that silly wabbit."

Bank Commercial

This is called a chord sheet, which is used frequently in the studio. The drums are given stylistic direction at the beginning of the chart and must create the groove, which, in this case, is a half-time funk shuffle (known today as hip-hop).

The band pushes can be caught, but don't let them interrupt the groove or flow of the piece. Watch the articulation and syncopation in bars 5 and 9.

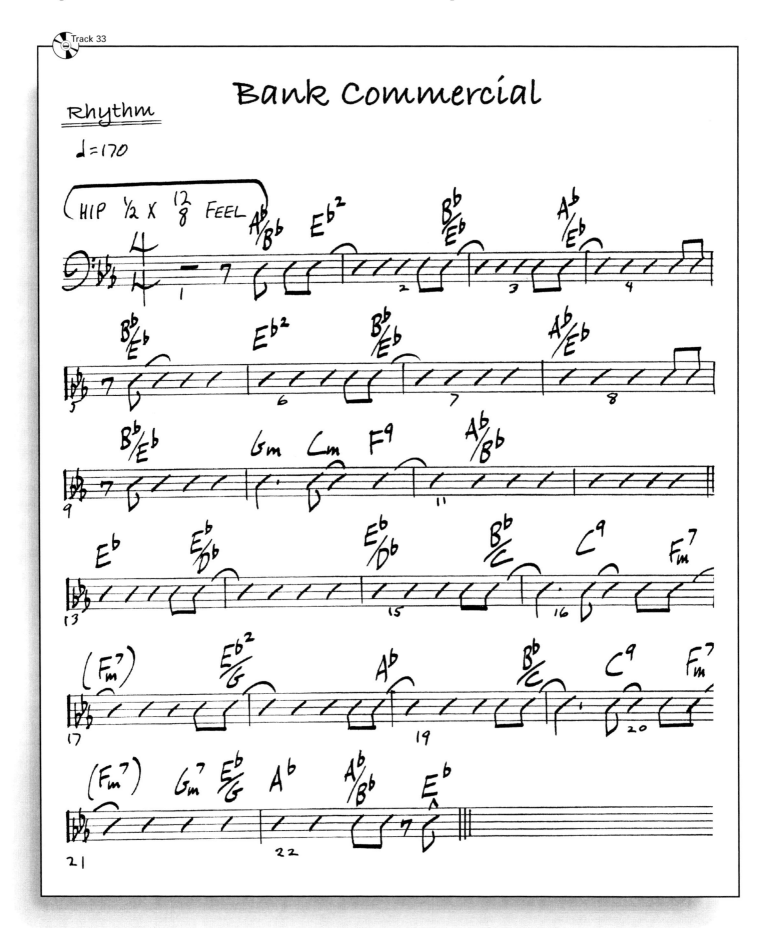

TV/Radio IDs

The next eight cues are quick identification spots (IDs) for TV or radio stations. You hear them constantly, but they're so short you don't ever think about them. They're quick, they're slick and they have a definite style. IDs range from 5–30 seconds long, which is not a sufficient amount of time to experiment finding a groove.

ID #1

The reading format here is called a master rhythm part in which the piano, bass, guitar and sometimes drums all read from the same part. Often there is no drum part, and the drummer is called upon to construct one with the information in the master part. The drummer must pay close attention to the harmonic rhythm, as it will help determine the bass drum part. The band kicks at bars ④, ⑤, ⑦ and ⑧ must be orchestrated to match the articulation of the band.

ID #2

The articulation in the first 2 bars sets the tone for the cue establishing a busy, bossa-rock feel. The 5/4 bar sneaks up on you, so be aware of the entire phrase (bars 3 – 6). At the end, the release or cutoff is on beat 1 (-1).

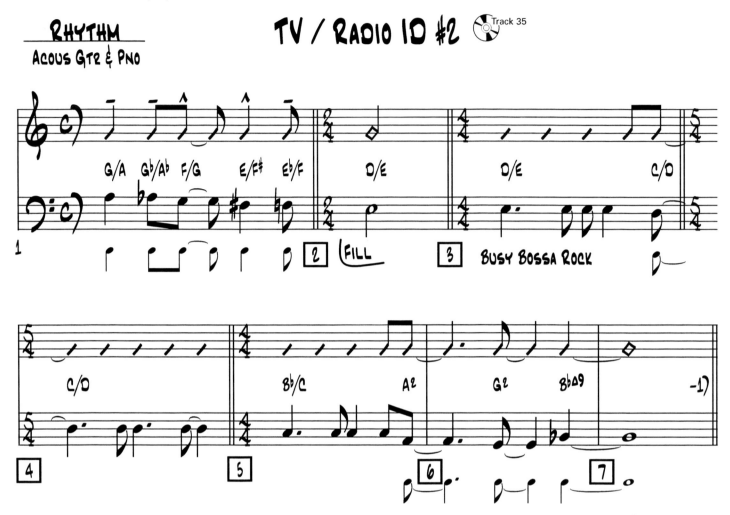

ID #3

This one is a quickie where you must have a groove ready to go. A "Big Two," which is similar to a half-time funk shuffle, is needed, with the bass part determining the bass drum part.

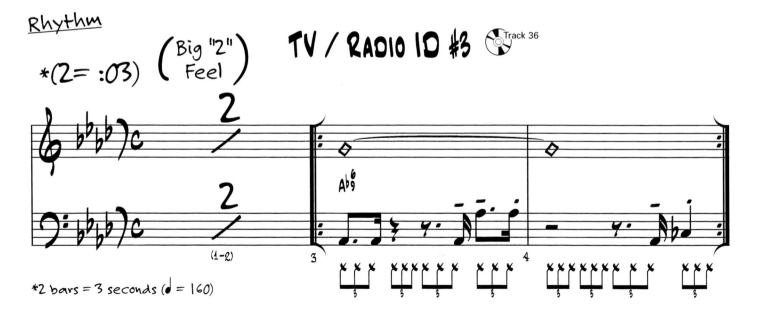

ID #4

This cue calls for a clean, effective reggae feel; make sure it works with the bass part. The last hit on the last sixteenth note of bar ③ releases on beat 3 of bar ④.

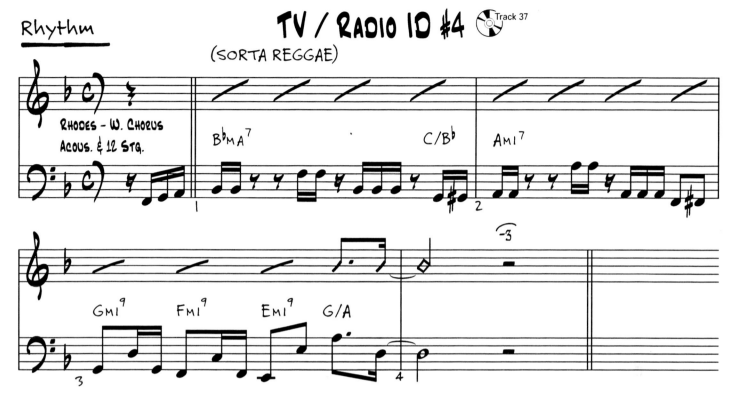

ID #5

The only way you could know the style or tempo of this cue is by knowing the referenced tune ("Lil' Darlin'"), a slow Basie jazz classic. Brushes or delicate sticks will work on this one. A sizzle cymbal might help the feel of this cue, providing a legato approach to the cymbals.

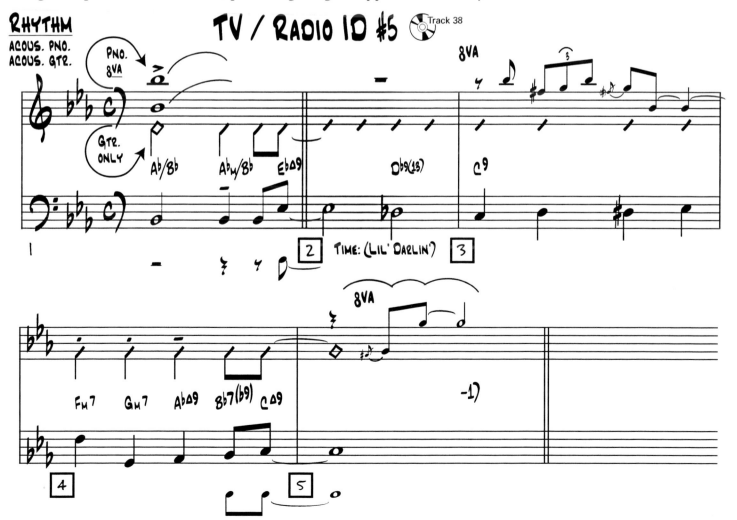

ID #6

The groove on this cue is referred to as an R&B strut feel, which utilizes a tight hi-hat bass drum concept with a tight 2 and 4. Watch the bass part.

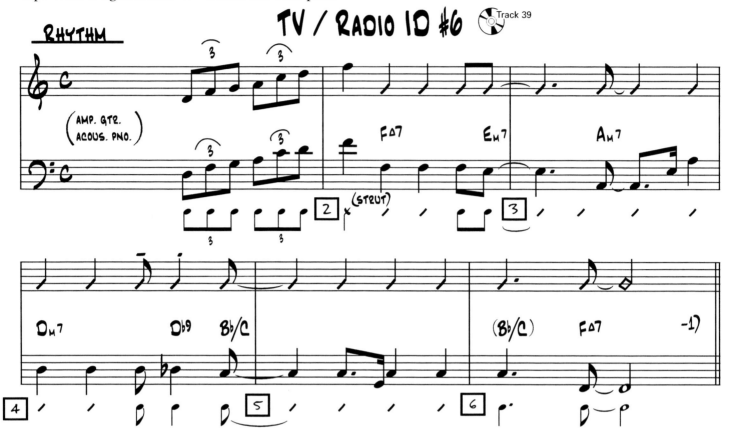

ID #7

This cue has some horn kicks written in (plus the rhythm parts), so there's almost a double-duty in the interpretation. There is no drum part, so just interpret it as a big band shout chorus, filling and setting up the kicks.

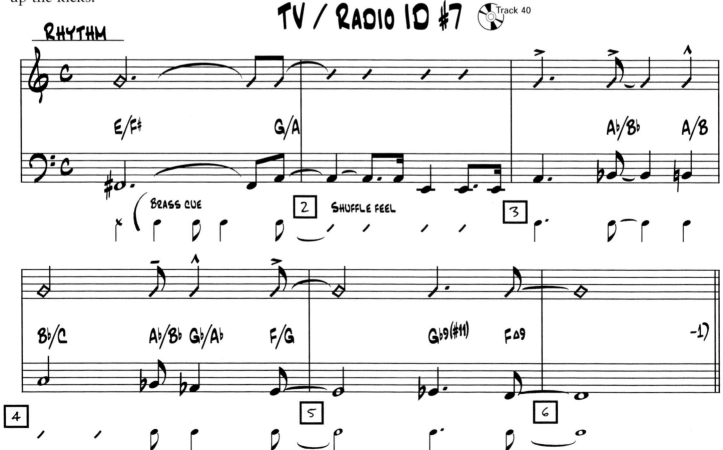

ID #8

The directions on this one are sketchy and say only "show feel." Don't get involved with the piano part but concentrate more on the bass part (rhythms). At bar 16, the part goes from two staves to one, with some unison kicks. In bar 22, the drums should play a fill "in the hole" to set up the last unison figure.

Chapter 7
DANCE JOBS

This chapter deals with what are frequently called "stock arrangements," which are charts used primarily in dance bands. Unfortunately, these arrangements are usually old, poorly written charts that can be confusing if you haven't seen them before. Because the charts can be very repetitive, it is a good idea to be familiar with the tune to keep from losing your place. Also, these types of charts tend to leave out band figures, forcing the player to use his/her ears. Don't be afraid to mark the parts.

Remember, the sole purpose of this music is for dancing. With that in mind, providing steady, danceable and simple time-keeping is a must. While playing dance music isn't an exercise in creativity, it most definitely requires skill. If you're going to be playing a lot of dance jobs, do some homework and listen to the old dance bands of Glenn Miller, Tommy Dorsey, Harry James, Ray Anthony, etc., to learn the style and the tempos. Taking some dance lessons from a good instructor is also highly recommended. Even an hour of instruction in each style will give you an awareness of effective tempos and the importance of clean playing.

PERFORMANCE NOTES/SUGGESTIONS

Choice Examples

The first two charts have no accompaniment tracks, but they represent the "look" of a stock dance band arrangement.

The first, a slow fox trot, actually has a vibe part written into the drum part. Absolutely no figures are written, only a few rolls at phrase points. As this is very typical, it is important to learn as many dance-job tunes as possible. Knowing the melody and form will make this type of reading much easier.

The second tune, a Latin selection, looks like a computer might be needed to figure out the drum key in the beginning. Don't ever get so wrapped up in reading these bizarre parts that you loose sight of the groove and the tempo/time. This is a good example of why it is important to develop a catalog of grooves and beats to fit these situations—so you are not held hostage by an unclear part.

One O'Clock Bump

On any given weekend, a tune similar to this one is probably played 10,000 times across the U.S., because it represents the World War II dance era to a large segment of the population. The player must listen to the original recordings of this style in order to solidify the concept. Backbeat seems to be the name of the game in this tune, for it just keeps loading on background figures. Again, a clear, simple ride pattern is needed, with filling kept to a minimum.

Cha-Cha Fuego

This big band cha-cha is standard fare at a dance job. The beat must be simple and clear for the dancers, and a cha-cha cowbell is highly recommended for this style.

It is always a good idea to listen to dance records to broaden your concept of what beats are effective for dancers. You will probably find the beats are very lean and the correct tempo is the most important element. If the tunes are at the wrong tempo or the groove is too cluttered, people won't dance. Save your songos, hip sambas and contemporary jazz licks for another setting.

String of Diamonds

This tune is similar to "String of Pearls" from the Glenn Miller library, which is an oft-requested tune from the big band era. The syncopations in the melody don't have to be caught; it's more important to keep steady time by using, perhaps, a cross-stick on beat four to begin with. The arrangement has a dynamic change (soft-loud) at the end, so make it happen.

In a Mood

This type of tune is considered a dance job standard and will probably be played on most big band dance gigs. Most important is to keep a nice, steady dance tempo with energy. You can't get too jazzy, and you must keep a simple ride vs. a "broken" jazz ride, being careful to avoid a lot of syncopated snare drum interplay.

There are a few band hits in the melody but, other than that, it is fairly straight ahead.

Slow Fox Trot

Drums   **Slow Fox Trot**

Samba

Drums

(SAMBA TEMPO)

INSTRUCTIONS AND KEY TO THIS PART:

1. ♩ = played with stick, right hand, near side of Sn. Dr. (Snares off)

2. ◻ = played with stick, right hand, in center of Sn. Dr. (Snares off)

3. ↑ or ✕ = played with brush, left hand, without lifting brush from drum head, using left hand also as damper for ◻ notes

4. Accent third beat of each bar on Bass Drum.

Track 42

ONE O'CLOCK BUMP

Drums

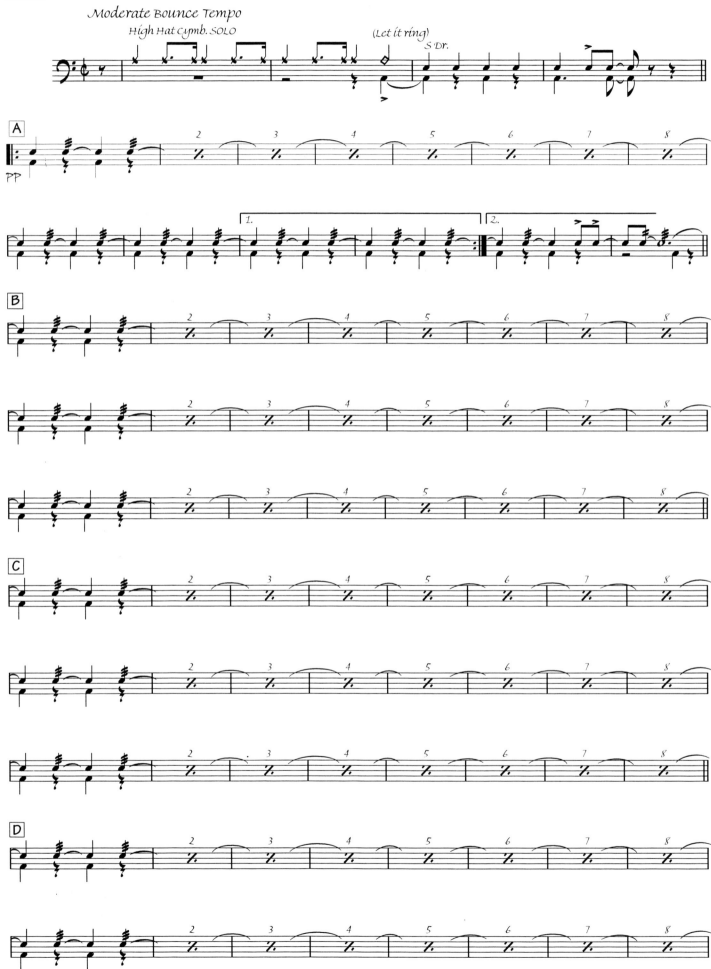

One O'Clock Bump   —2—

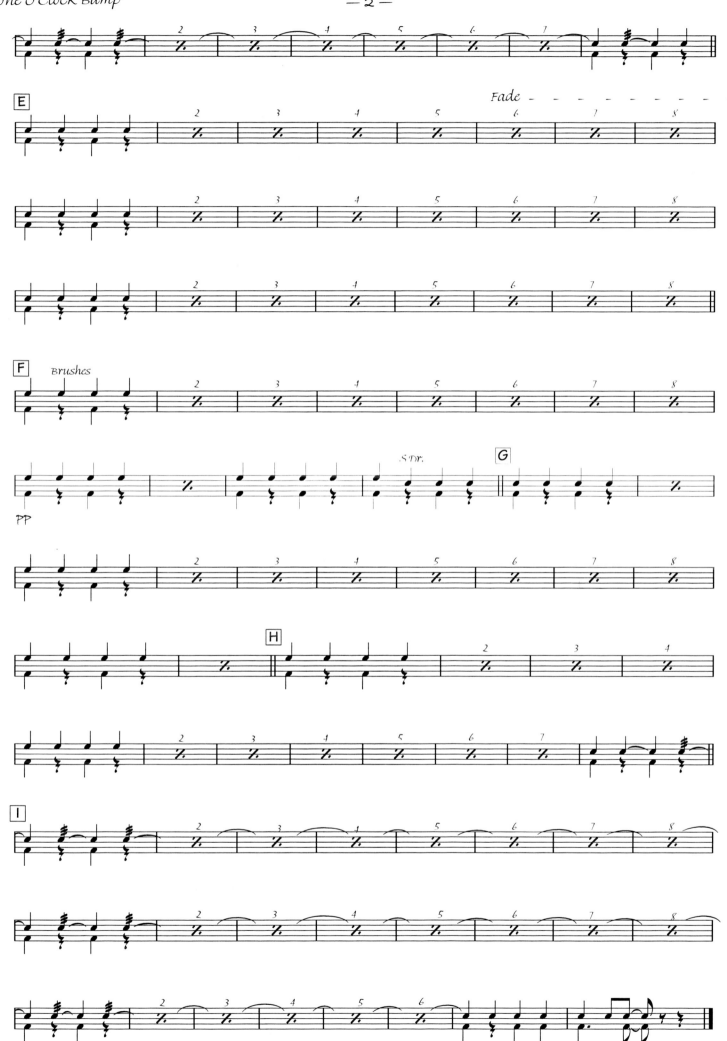

Track 43

Cha-Cha Fuego

Arranged by
Tom Warrington &
Steve Houghton

<u>Drums</u>

♩ = 126

Solo — — — — — — — —

[A] Cha-Cha

Fill — — — — —

[B] Time

[C]

Fill & Fade — — — —

Track 44

String Of Diamonds

Drums

Track 45